Ed Emberley's Complete FunPrint Drawing Book

LITTLE, BROWN AND COMPANY

New York ❧ Boston

CONTENTS

Easy! Fun!

You can make FunPrints using your fingers or your thumbs. Use just the tip to make small prints.

1. Press your finger on an ink pad

or paint it with watercolor and a brush.

2. Press it on your paper.

3. Let it dry.

4. Draw.

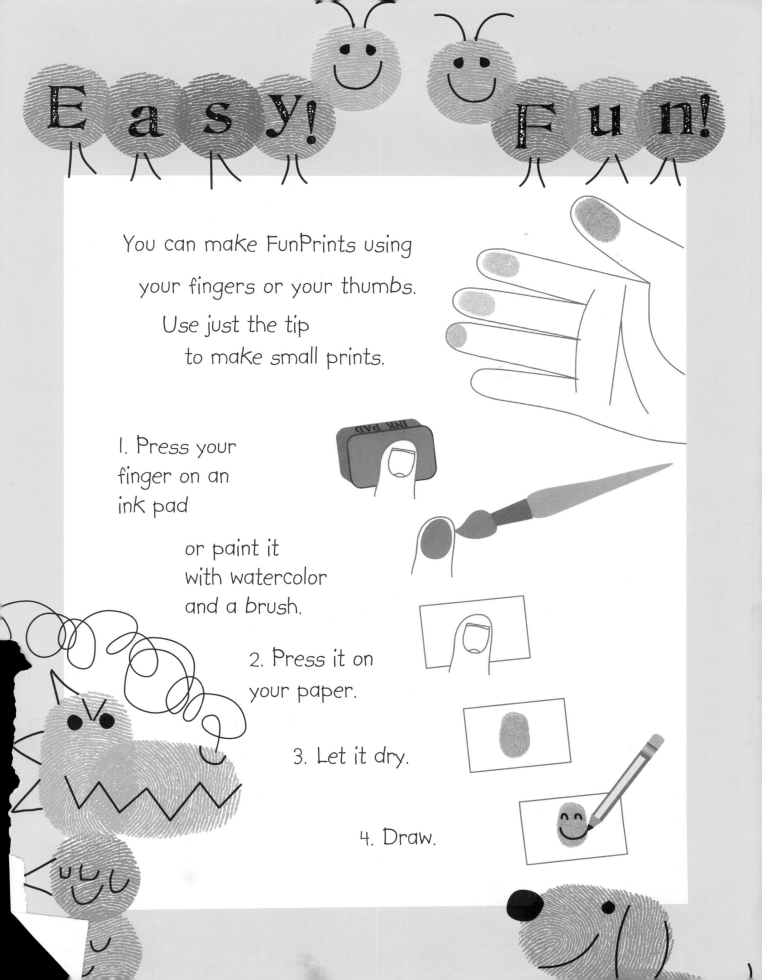

PERSON

(JUST A LINE CAN MAKE A HAT.)

WALKING

FISH

BIRD

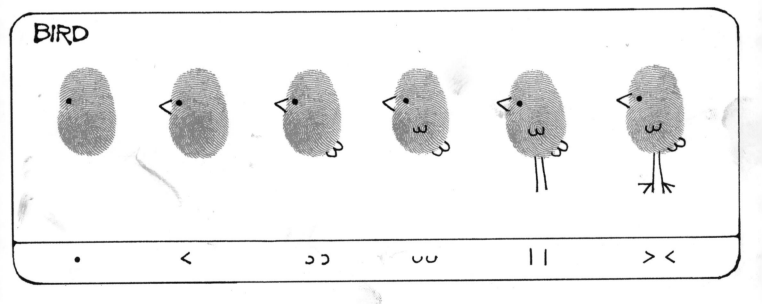

SPIDER

RABBIT

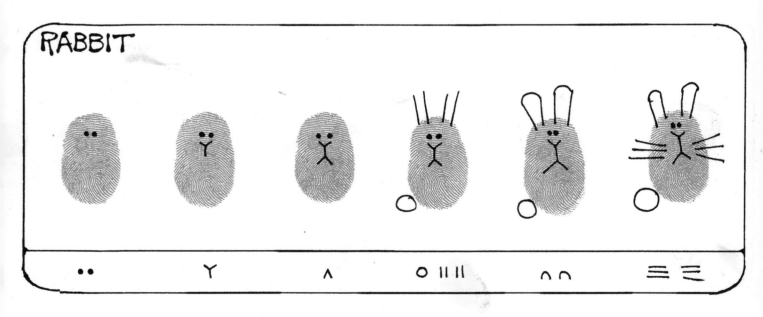

6

HALLOWEEN

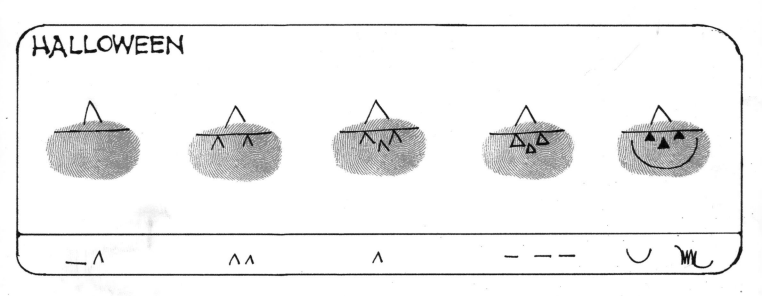

FROG

HAPPY
•• ∪

NOT HAPPY
•• ∩

LAUGHING
∩∩ ∪ —

ANGRY
•• ∩ ∨

SLY
•• ∪ ∨

WORRIED
•• ∩ ∧

SHY
•• ∪ ∧

SPEAKING
•• ∪ —

WINKING
∪ • —

8

SHOUTING

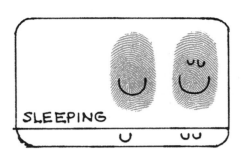

SLEEPING

WHISTLING

SCARED

SINGING

SMILING

CRYING

OTHERS

9

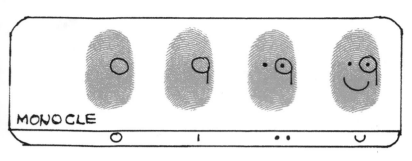

MONOCLE

O   I   ..   ∪

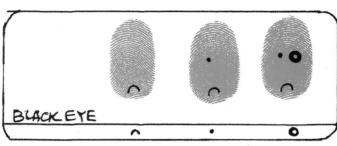

BLACK EYE

∧   .   ⊙

GLASSES

OO   – – –   ..   ∪

LOOKING AROUND

SUNGLASSES

PIRATE

═   ∪   ∿   .   ∪   >   \   ⁞⁚⁚

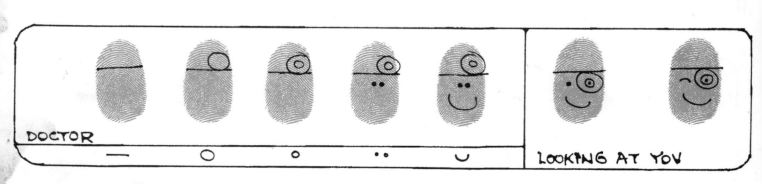

DOCTOR

—   O   ∘   ..   ∪

LOOKING AT YOU

10

CROOK

=   O   O   ·· ⌒   m   C   >   — o

OTHERS

HAIR

SCRIBBLES MAKE GOOD HAIR, WHISKERS, SKIRTS AND SHAGGY DOGS.

HERE ARE SOME MORE SCRIBBLES AND SOME SPECKS AND SCRATCHES.

HATS

CAP

HATS

COWBOY — ( ) COWGIRL

FOOTBALL —) ( ) (|| SIDE VIEW

FIREMAN — ( ) / o

SKI CAPS — — o ETC.

ADMIRAL

SAILOR

TURBAN

BAND PERSON

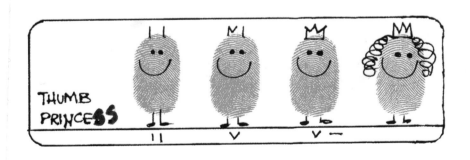

THUMB PRINCESS

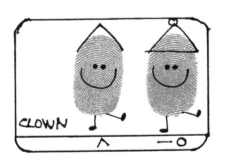

CLOWN

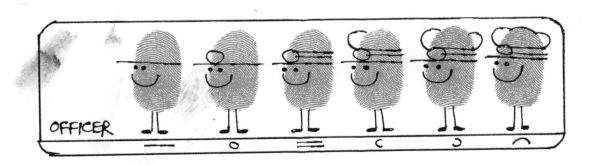

OFFICER

13

ACTION

WALKING

WALKING OVER THAT WAY→

BACK VIEW

←

SIDE VIEW

RUNNING

KICKING

JUMPING

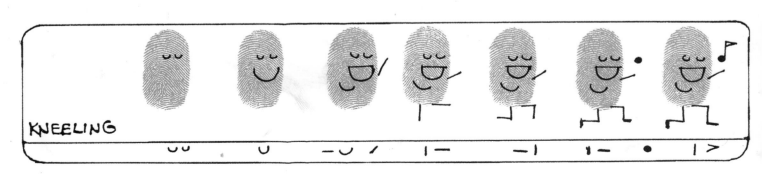

KNEELING

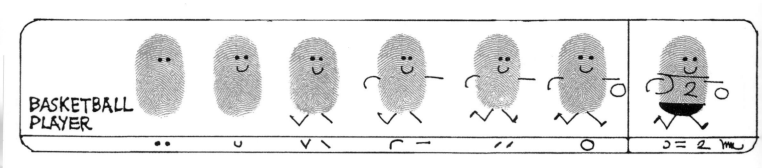

BASKETBALL PLAYER

SURFER

ETC. ETC.

BOXING

ETC.

ANIMAL ACTION

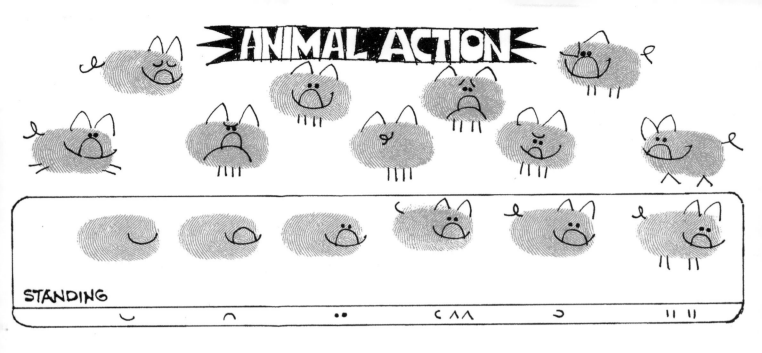

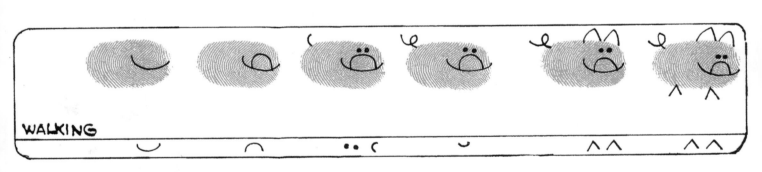

STANDING

WALKING

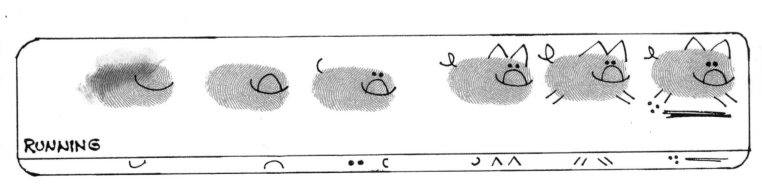

RUNNING

17

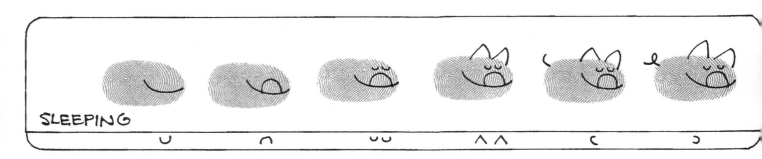

SLEEPING

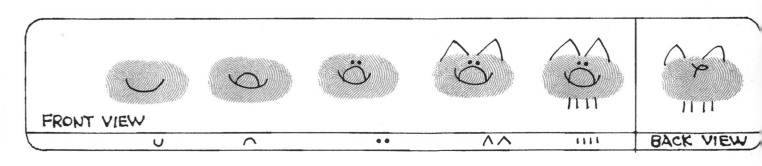

FRONT VIEW   BACK VIEW

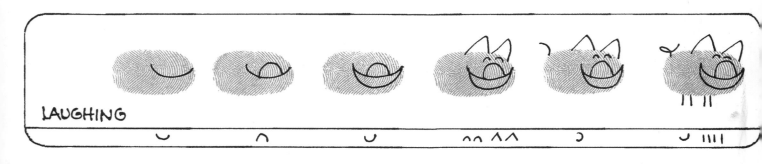

LAUGHING

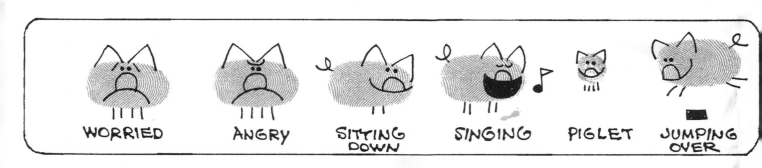

WORRIED   ANGRY   SITTING DOWN   SINGING   PIGLET   JUMPING OVER

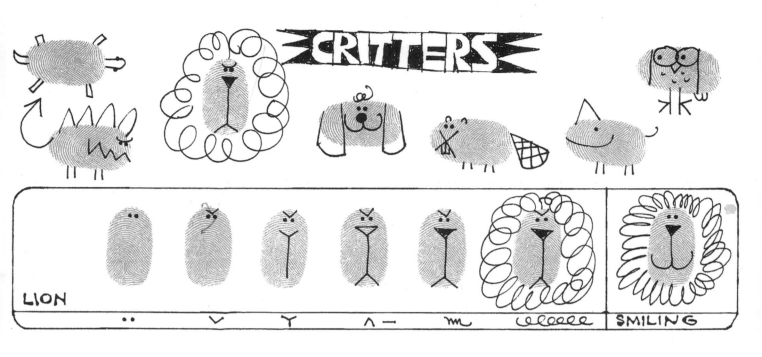

CRITTERS

| LION | .. | ⌄ | Y | ∧ − | ⌢⌢⌢ | ꬳꬳꬳꬳꬳ | SMILING |

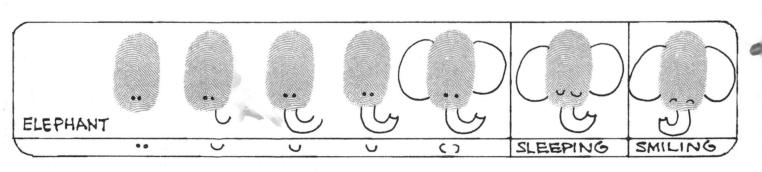

| CAT | .. | ⌣ | ∪∪ | − ∧∧ | ∪ ∪∪ ∪∪ | ≡ ≡ | WINKING |

| ELEPHANT | .. | ∪ | ∪ | ∪ | ( ) | SLEEPING | SMILING |

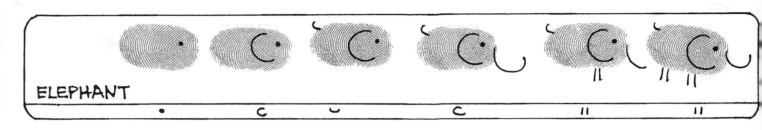

ELEPHANT

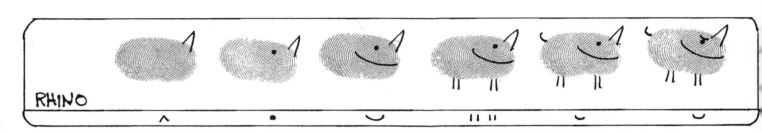

RHINO

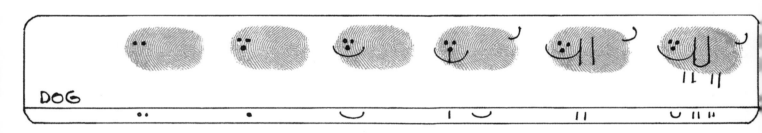

DOG

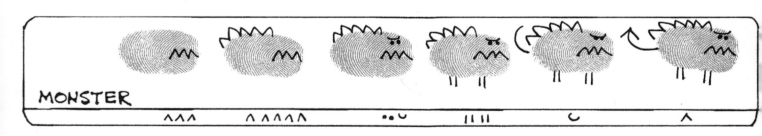

MONSTER

BEAVER

OWL

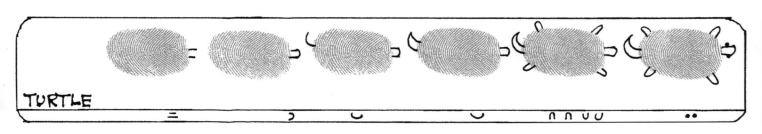

TURTLE

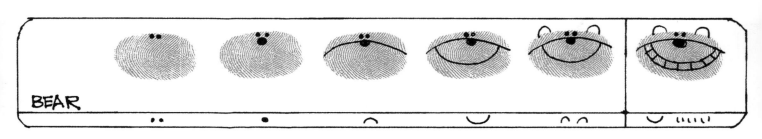

BEAR

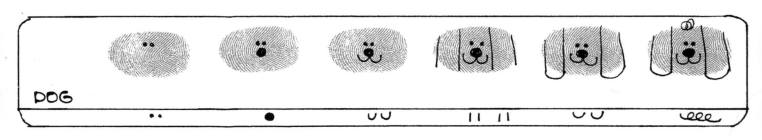

DOG

HAMSTER

HAMSTER TOP VIEW

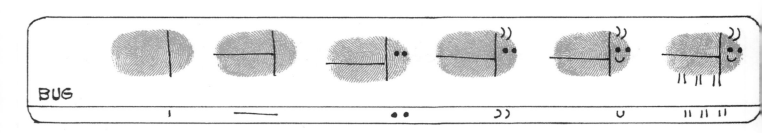

BUG

BEE

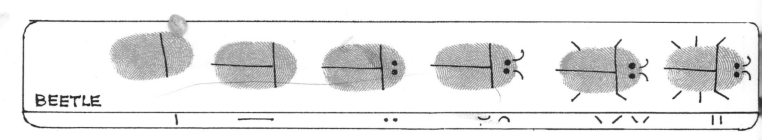

BEETLE

CATERPILLAR

BIRDS

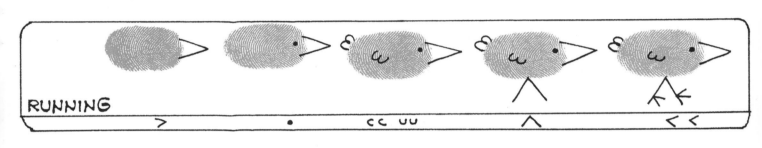

STANDING

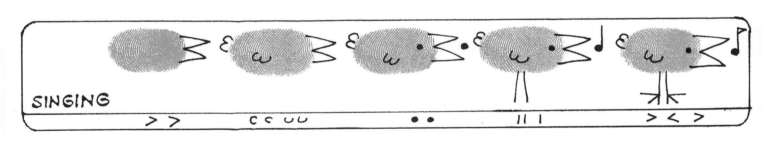

RUNNING

SINGING

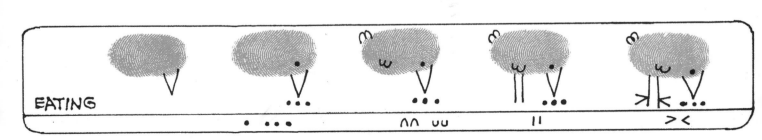

EATING

23

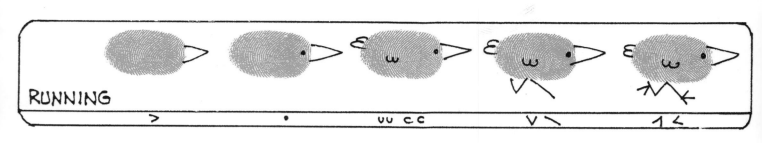

RUNNING

>   •   ʊʊ cc   ʌ⅃   ⅂⅄

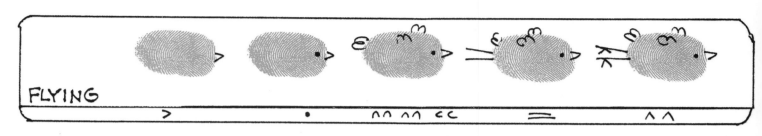

FLYING

>   •   ʌʌ ʌʌ cc   =   ʌʌ

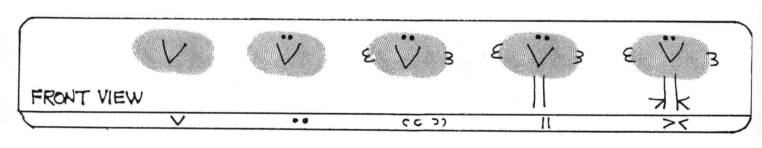

SLEEPING   NEST

>   ʊ   cc   ʊʊ   ≡≡—≡

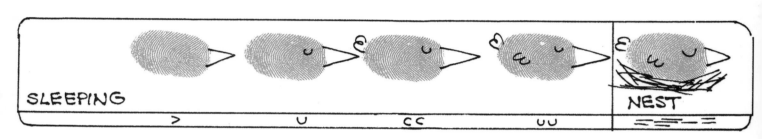

FRONT VIEW

V   ••   cc ɔɔ   ‖   ✕

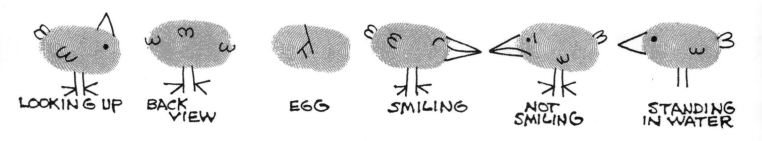

LOOKING UP   BACK VIEW   EGG   SMILING   NOT SMILING   STANDING IN WATER

24

HOLIDAYS

SANTA

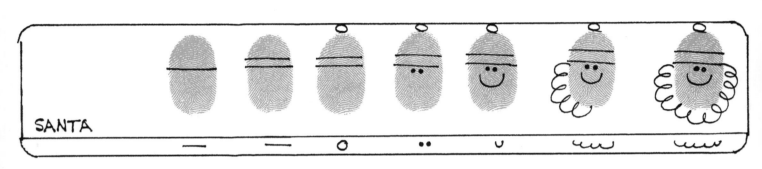

FIRECRACKER

BIRTHDAY CAKE

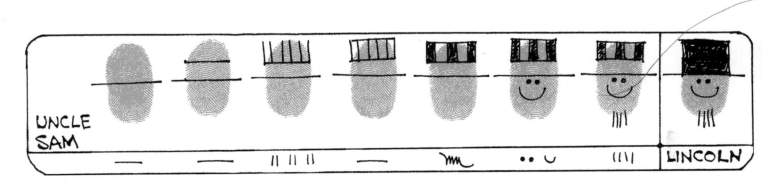

UNCLE SAM

LINCOLN

HALLOWEEN

HALLOWEEN

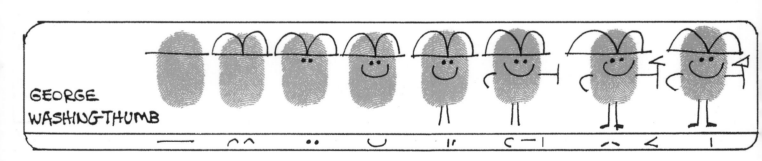

GEORGE
WASHING-THUMB

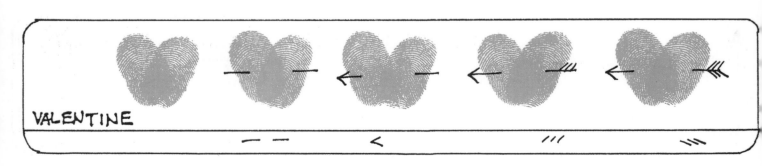

VALENTINE

26

PILGRIM

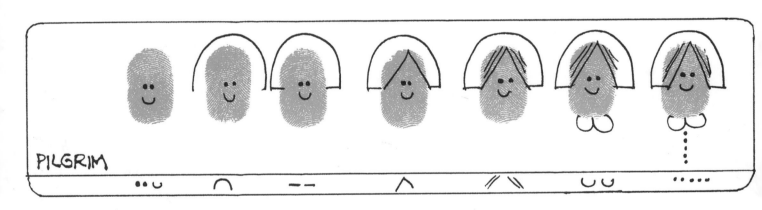

PILGRIM

EASTER BUNNY

MORE THUMBS

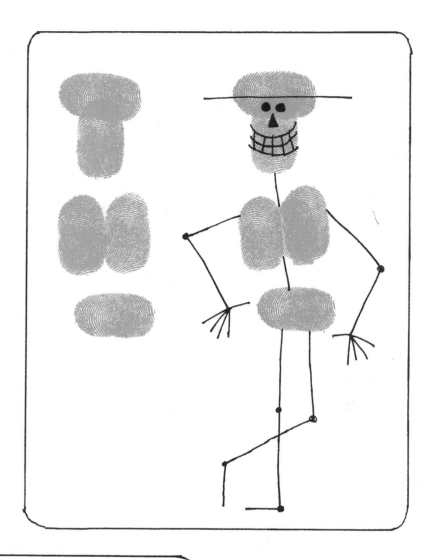

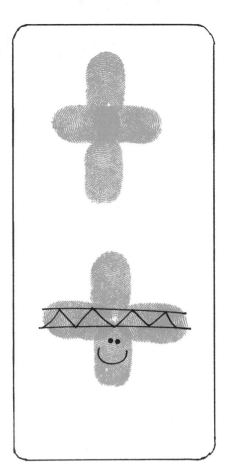

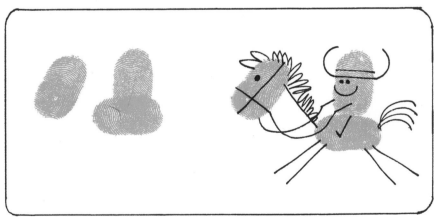

THIS AND THAT

THE GARDEN

FLOWER

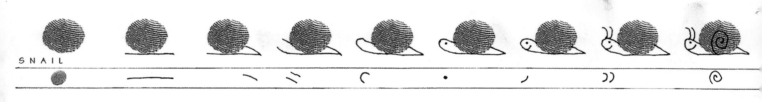

SNAIL

FROG

34

SMALL FLOWER   CROCUS   TULIP

BROWN ANT   CATERPILLAR   CENTIPEDE

BUMBLEBEE

THE POND

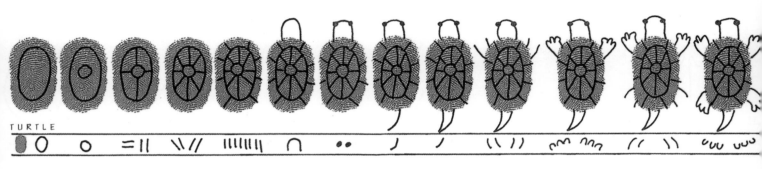

TURTLE

DUCK

POLLYWOG

BUTTERFLY

SWIMMING FROG

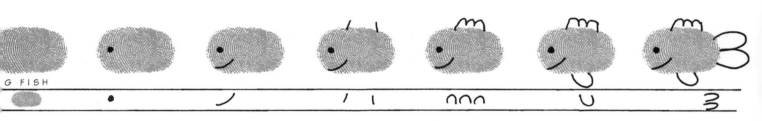

G FISH

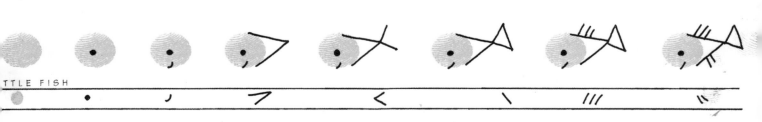

TTLE FISH

37

FINGERLINGS

I ALSO CALL THESE MY TEENY TINIES. I USE A DIFFERENT FINGERTIP FOR EACH COLOR.

SPRING

SUMMER

RABBIT

MOUSE

OWL

FROG

DOG

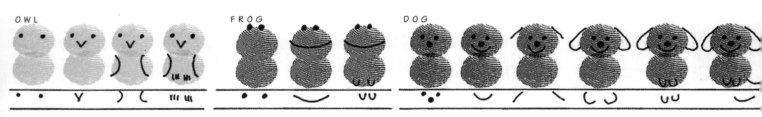

BEAVER

FALL

FALL

WINTER

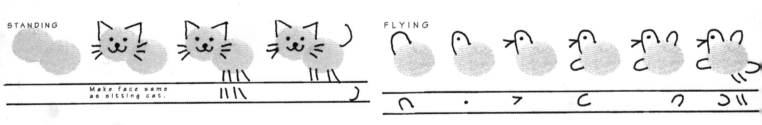

SITTING CAT

BIRD

STANDING

Make face same
as sitting cat.

FLYING

RUNNING

Make face same
as sitting cat.

PECKING

ANIMALS

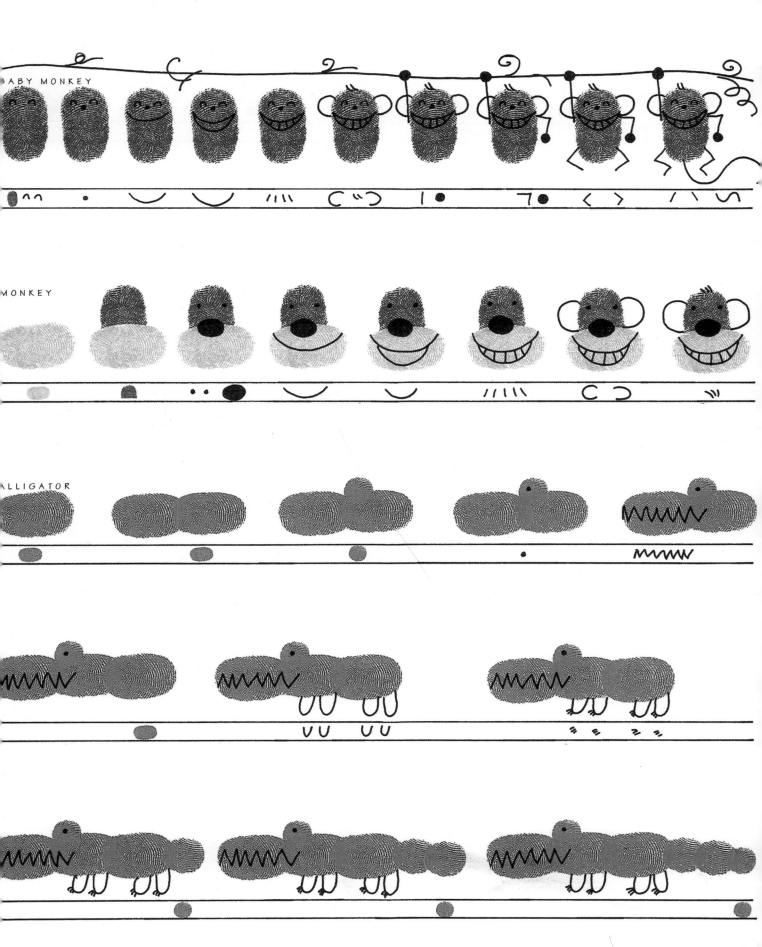

BABY MONKEY

MONKEY

ALLIGATOR

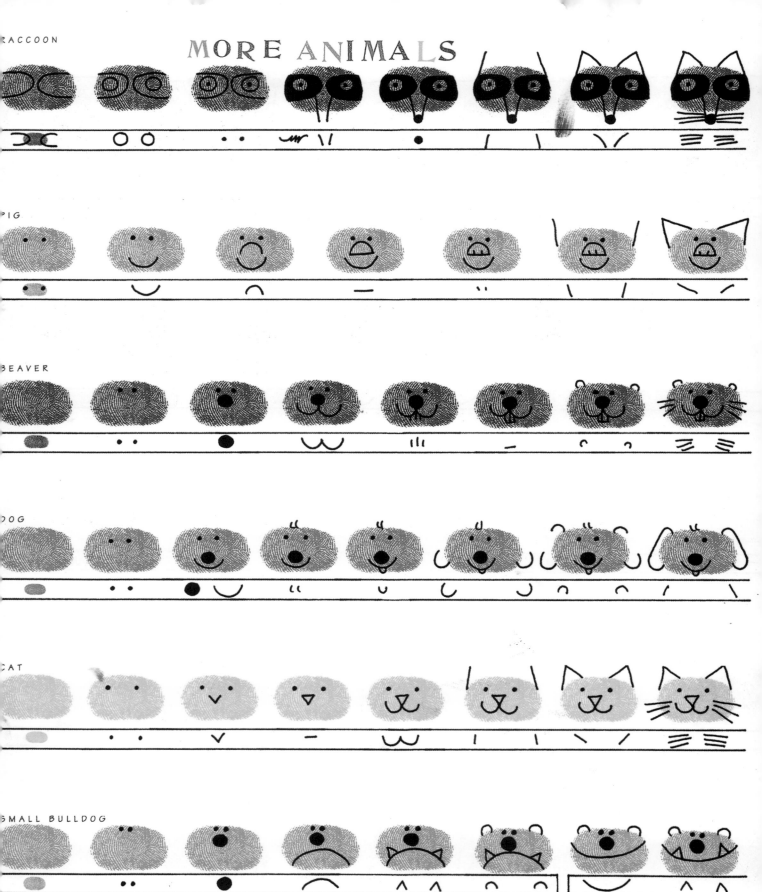

RACCOON

PIG

BEAVER

DOG

CAT

SMALL BULLDOG

MOUSE

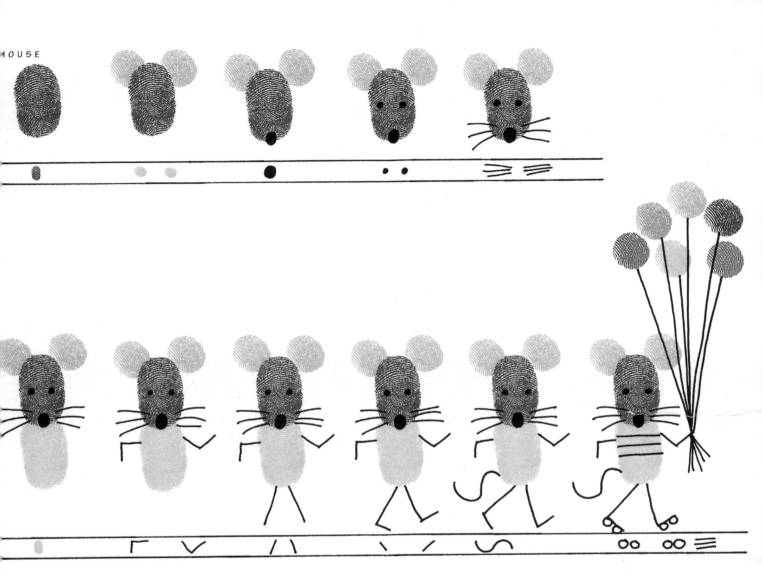

BIG BULLDOG

BIRDS

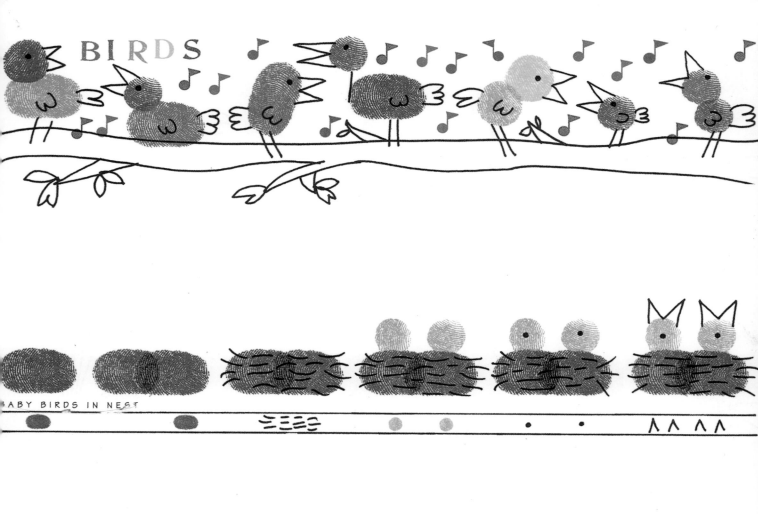

BABY BIRDS IN NEST

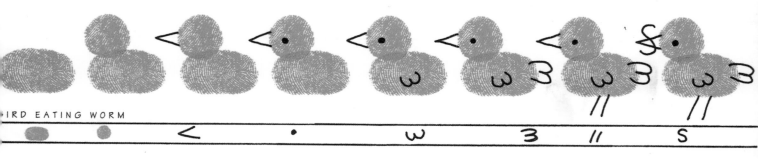

BIRD EATING WORM

BIRD FRONT VIEW   BIRD BACK VIEW

BIRD FLYING

BIRD SINGING

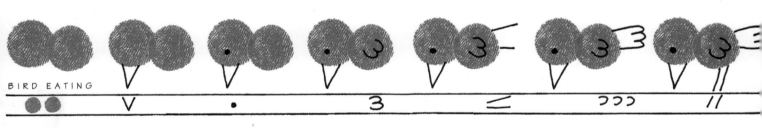

BIRD EATING

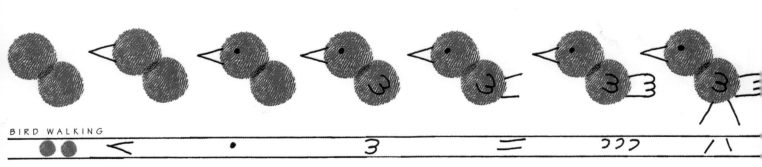

BIRD WALKING

BEAN BUDDIES

I THINK FINGERPRINTS LOOK LIKE LITTLE BEANS. I LIKE TO USE THESE LITTLE "FINGER BEANS" TO MAKE ALL DIFFERENT KINDS OF LITTLE BEAN BUDDIES.

BASIC

PEA BEAN BUDDY   BAKED BEAN BUDDY   LIMA BEAN BUDDY   JELLY BEAN BUDDY

SPEAKING

POINTING   LOOK

YAWNING   HO HUM

CELEBRATING   HOORAY!

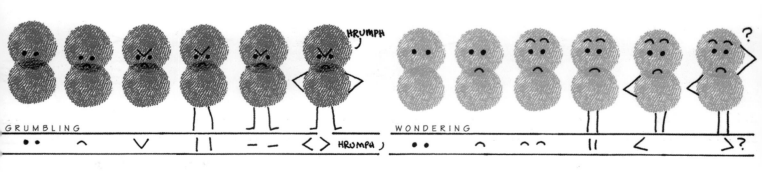

GRUMBLING   HRUMPH

WONDERING

46

WALKING

JOGGING

RUNNING

WINNING

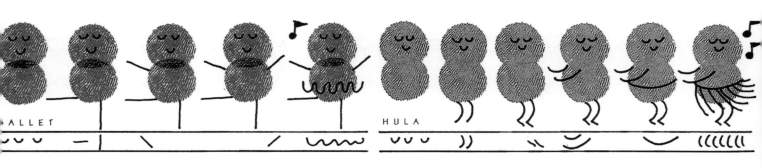

BALLET

HULA

CLOG DANCING

TAP DANCING

LITTLE CLOWN

NAPOLEON

SAILOR

QUEEN

KING

PRINCE

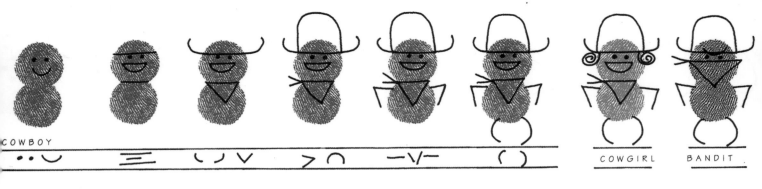

COWBOY

COWGIRL   BANDIT

PIRATE

SUPERPERSON

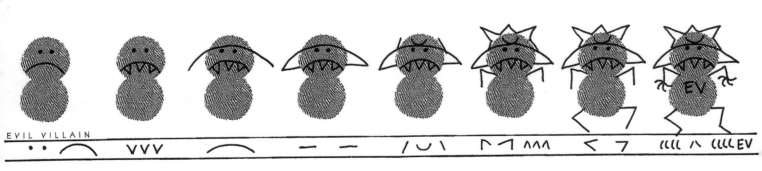

EVIL VILLAIN

FEELINGS

HAPPY

VERY HAPPY

VERY VERY HAPPY

SNOOTY

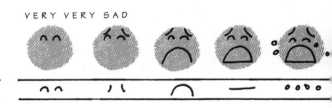

SAD

VERY SAD

VERY VERY SAD

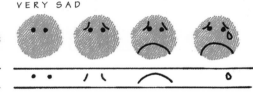

UPSET

ANGRY

VERY ANGRY

VERY VERY ANGRY

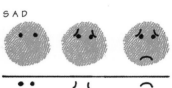

SLY (MISCHIEVOUS)

SHY (EMBARRASSED)

SUSPICIOUS

HURTING

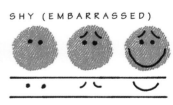

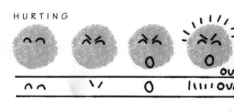

MUSIC

HUMMING

WHISTLING

SINGING

SINGERS

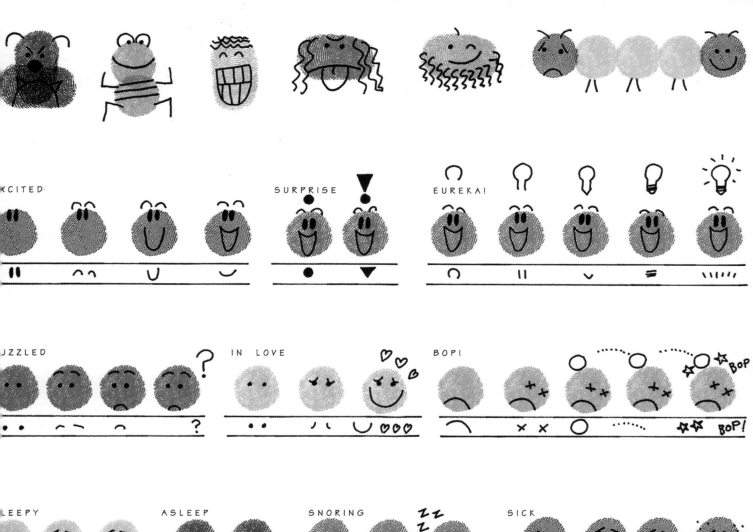

EXCITED

SURPRISE !

EUREKA!

PUZZLED

IN LOVE

BOP! BOP!

SLEEPY

ASLEEP

SNORING ZZZ

SICK

COLD

HOT

HELP! HELP!

HUNGRY YUM YUM

YUK!

PHOOEY!

YUM YUM

HELP!

BOP!

ZZZ

51

SPRING FUN

SKIPPING ROPE

BICYCLING

SKATEBOARDING

ROLLER-SKATING

APRIL SHOWERS

SHING

IKING

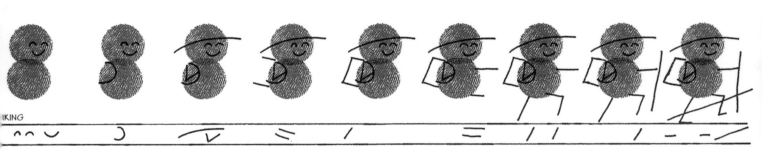

ITES

SUMMER FUN

CHASING BUTTERFLIES

SWIMMING

SURFING

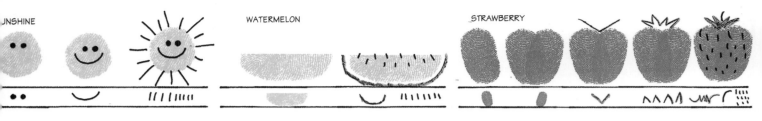

SUNSHINE   WATERMELON   STRAWBERRY

LAWN MOWING

SUNBATHING

BASEBALL

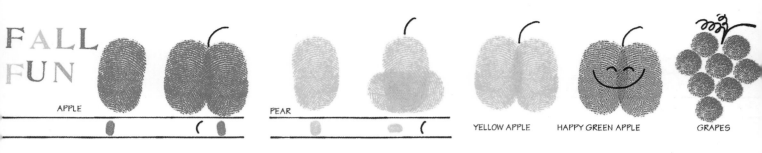

FALL
FUN

APPLE PEAR YELLOW APPLE HAPPY GREEN APPLE GRAPES

FARMING

LACROSSE

SOCCER

56

FOOTBALL

SPORTS FAN

CHEERLEADER

BASKETBALL

WINTER FUN

PENGUIN FRONT VIEW

PENGUIN SIDE VIEW

SNOWPERSON

KIING

KATING

OCKEY

59

HOLIDAYS

EASTER BUNNY

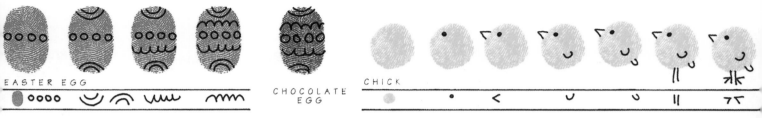

EASTER EGG

CHOCOLATE EGG

CHICK

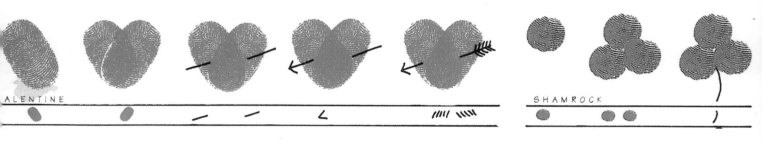

VALENTINE

SHAMROCK

LEPRECHAUN

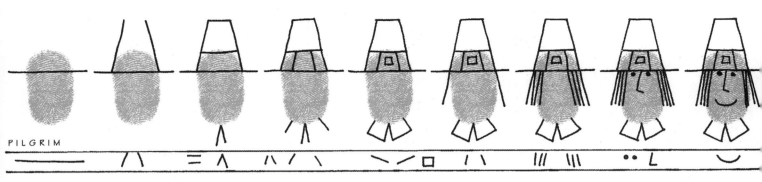

PILGRIM

TURKEY

PILGRIM

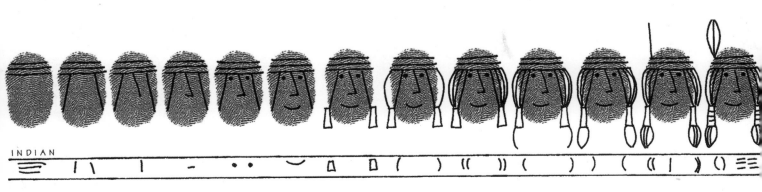

INDIAN

61

HALLOWEEN

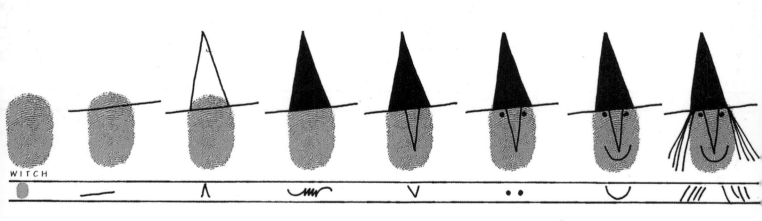

WITCH

FLYING WITCH

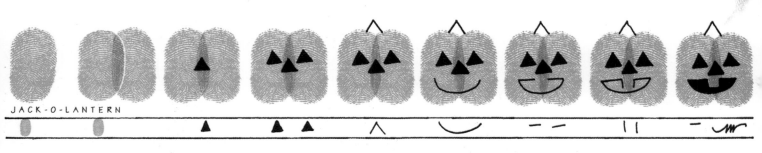

JACK-O-LANTERN

BAT

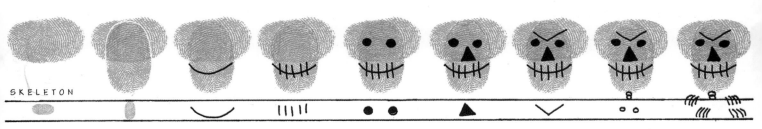

SKELETON

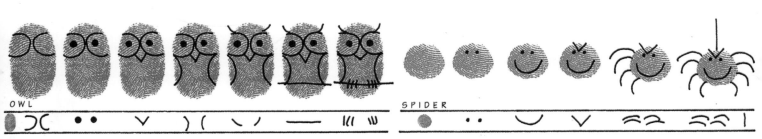

OWL

SPIDER

CAT

63

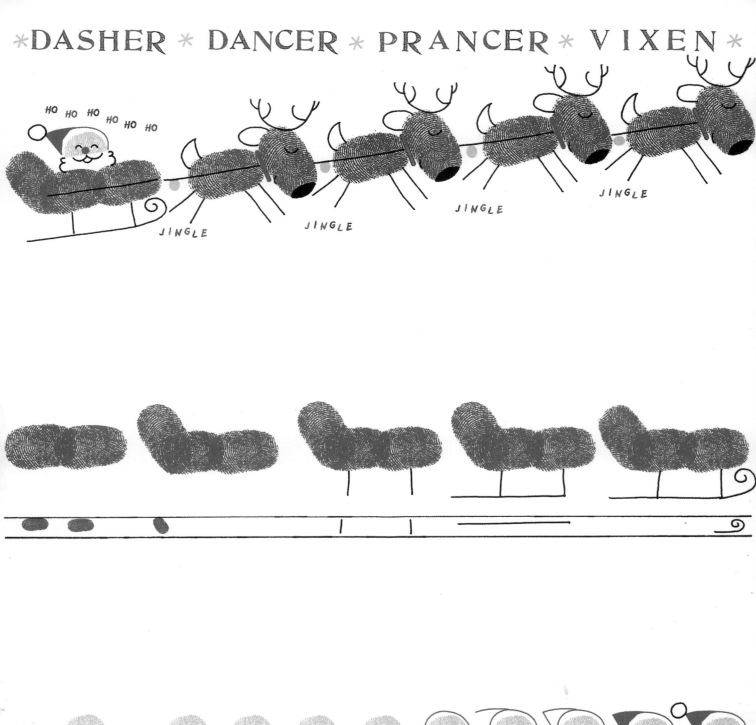

JINGLE JINGLE JINGLE

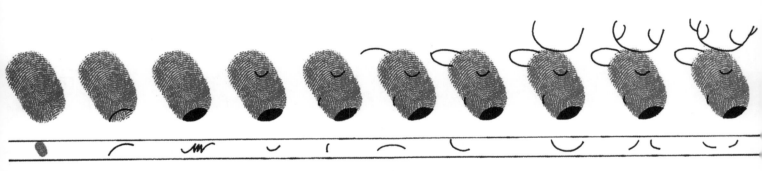

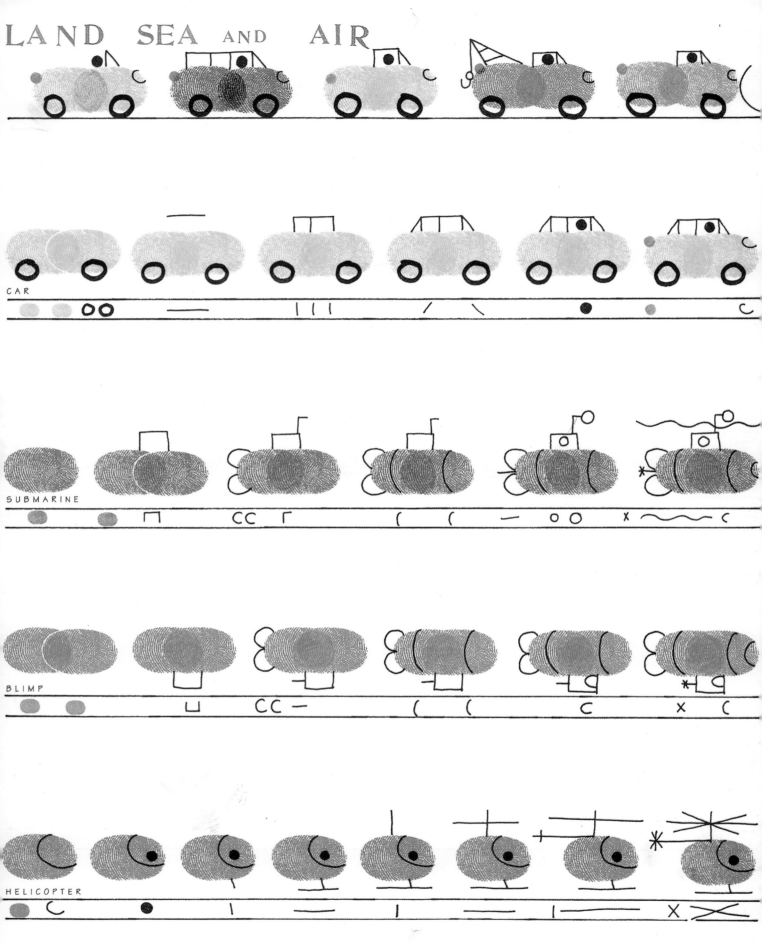

LAND SEA AND AIR

CAR

SUBMARINE

BLIMP

HELICOPTER

66

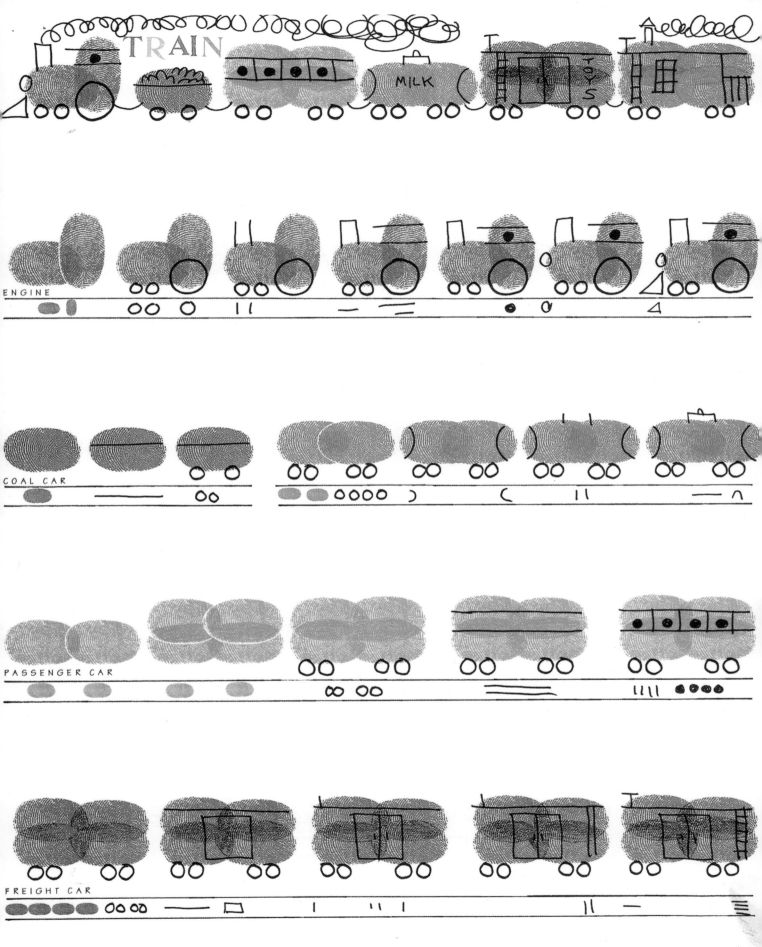

TRAIN

ENGINE

COAL CAR

PASSENGER CAR

FREIGHT CAR

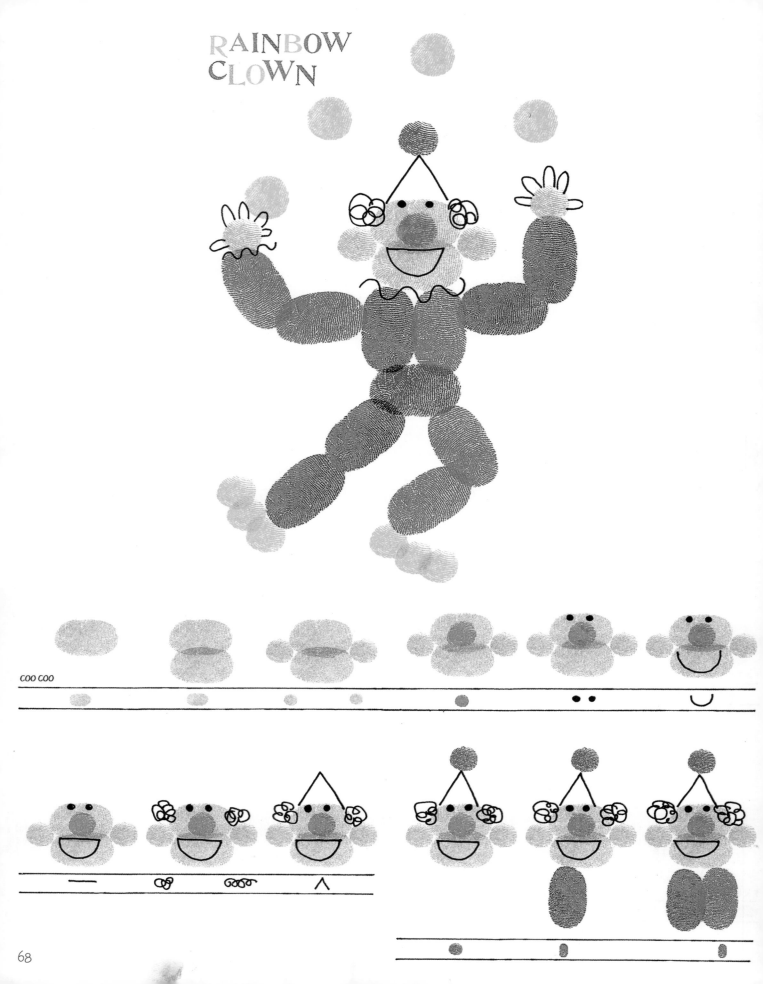

COO COO

FESTER

LULU

RAINBOW DRAGON

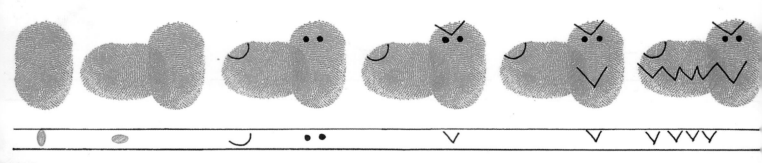

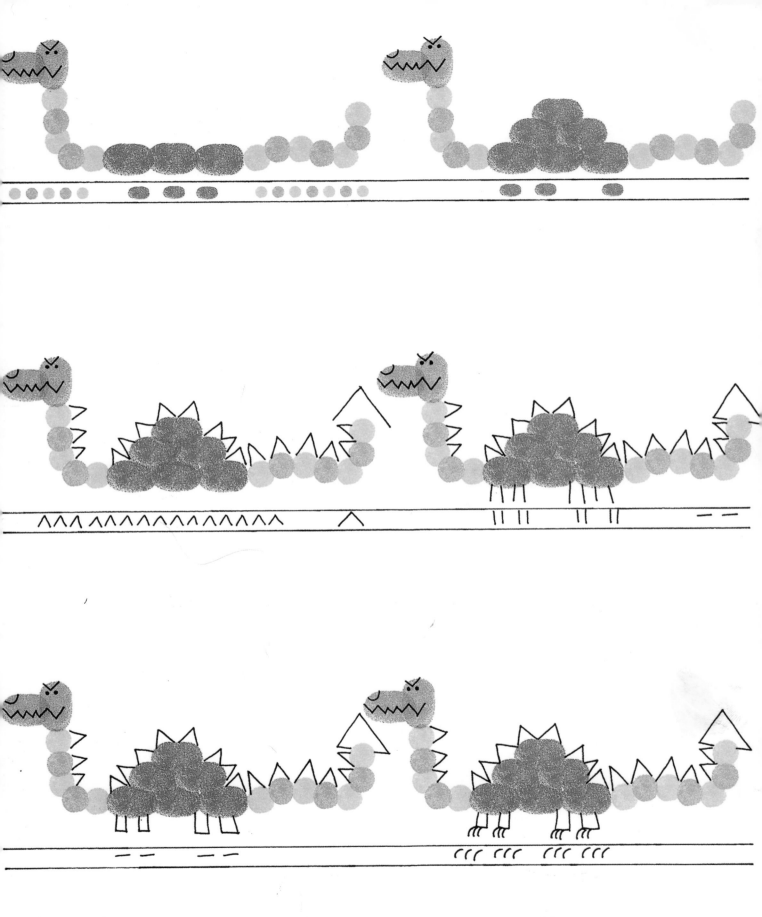

LION

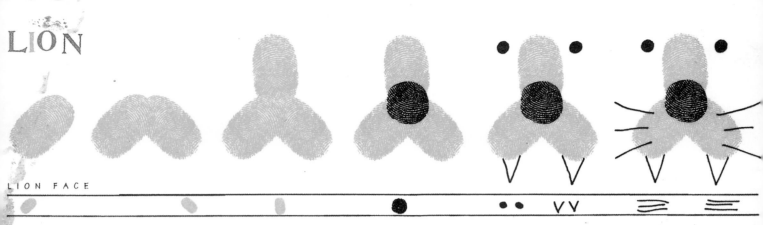

LION FACE

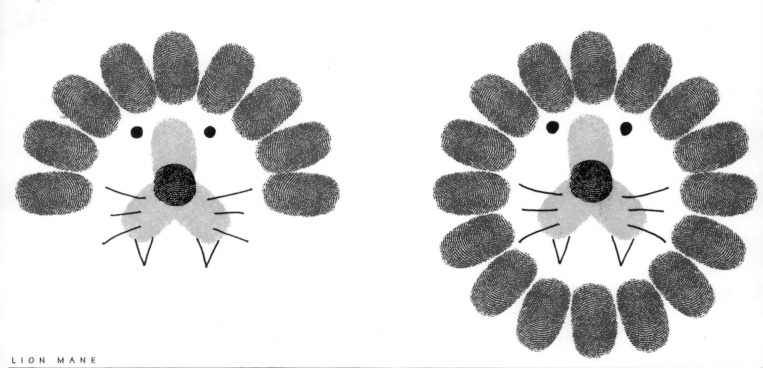

LION MANE

SKETCH BOOK

HERE ARE SOME FINGERPRINT THINGS I COULD NOT FIT INTO THIS BOOK. CAN YOU FIGURE OUT HOW I MADE THEM?

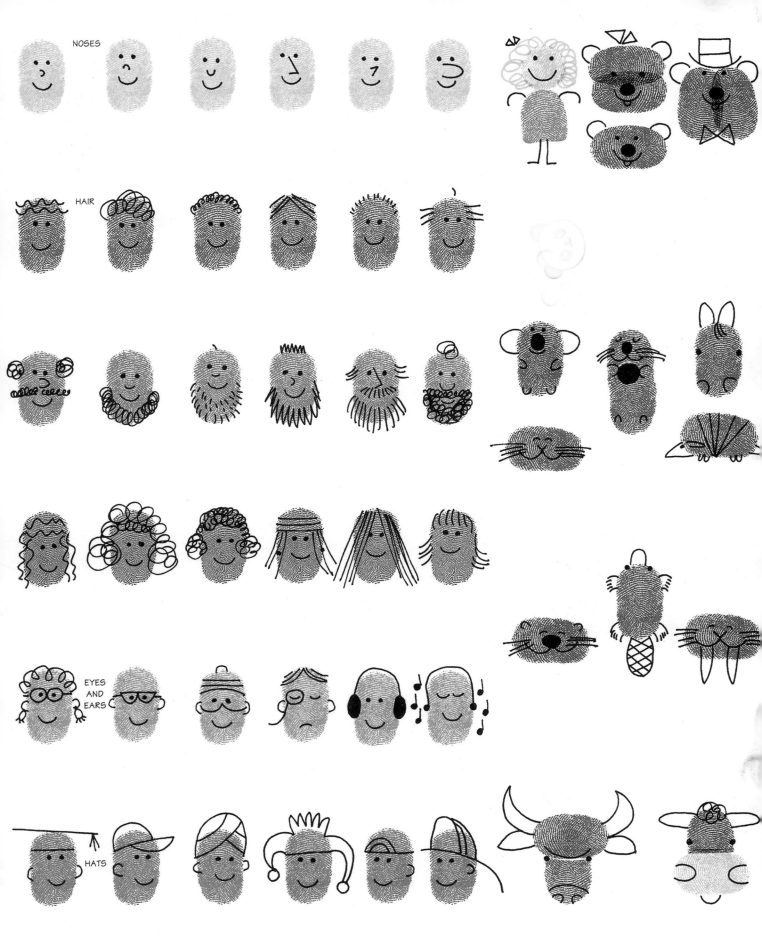

NOSES

HAIR

EYES
AND
EARS

HATS

75

ADVANCED FINGER-PRINTING

FOR THE ADVENTUROUS—
JUST A FEW OTHER WAYS TO COMBINE PRINTS,
COLORS, SIMPLE LINES, AND SOME
IMAGINATION TO MAKE PICTURES.
THERE ARE LOTS LEFT FOR YOU TO DISCOVER.
HAPPY DISCOVERING!

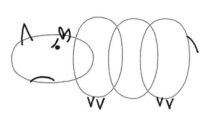

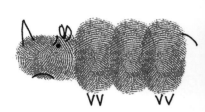

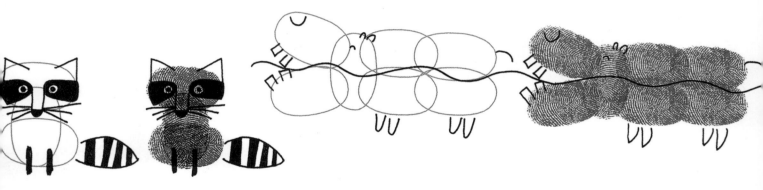

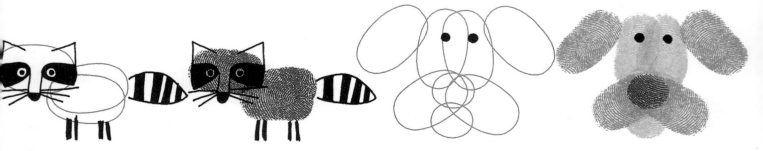

Something very special.

Just as no two fingerprints look just alike, no two fingerprint pictures will ever look just alike. Prints will be lighter or darker, lines will be thicker or thinner, colors will be different.

That means that no other fingerprint pictures will look just like the ones in this book, or just like yours. That's what will make your pictures "something very special."

More
Ed Emberley
Drawing Book
Fun!

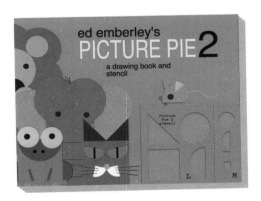

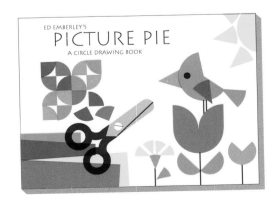

ED EMBERLEY'S DRAWING BOOK
OF ANIMALS

ED EMBERLEY'S DRAWING BOOK
OF FACES

ED EMBERLEY'S PICTURE PIE,
A CUT AND PASTE DRAWING BOOK

ED EMBERLEY'S PICTURE PIE TWO,
A DRAWING BOOK AND STENCIL

THE WING ON A FLEA:
A BOOK ABOUT SHAPES

ED EMBERLEY'S DRAWING BOOK,
MAKE A WORLD

ED EMBERLEY'S
BIG GREEN DRAWING BOOK
ED EMBERLEY'S
BIG ORANGE DRAWING BOOK
ED EMBERLEY'S
BIG PURPLE DRAWING BOOK
ED EMBERLEY'S BIG
RED DRAWING BOOK

DINOSAURS, A DRAWING BOOK
BY MICHAEL EMBERLEY

Little Brown and Company
Time Warner Book Group
1271 Avenue of the Americas, New York, NY 10020
Visit our Web site at www.lb-kids.com

First Edition

From the previously published books by Ed Emberley
GREAT THUMBPRINT DRAWING BOOK (copyright © 1977)
and
THE FINGERPRINT DRAWING BOOK (copyright © 2000)

ISBN 0-316-17448-3

10 9 8 7 6 5

SC

Manufactured in China